I0107437

A Bag of Badgers

And Other Poems

By

Casey McGovern

For my daughter and my wife,

Without whom,

This would probably be

A much more boring book

About a much more boring life.

Table of Contents

1. I Made You a Drink

I made you something:
  It's a little drink.

Tastier than tea,
  Milkier than milk,
    Inkier than ink
And salty as the sea.

It has a little flower petal
  And a flick of feather dust.
    A tiny bit of lake water,
      Just a pinch of rust.

      You said a whale is strengthened by the plankton,
      You said a horse is strengthened by its hay.

  So I made you a drink
    That has all that stuff and more.

  Go on.
  Try it.
I can wait all day.

2. Slime

Hey!
  I'm an awesome snail!
    I'm selling slime
  From a little pail!

The sort of slime
  That helps you slide
    On every kind of thing
  Outside!

Don't walk away!
  I'm here to stay!
    I'll catch up with you!
      One day...

3. Peace and Joy

We don't have a turkey
  At the winter feast,
    'Cause it's mean to eat
  A living thing,
    Mean to say the least.

So we gather together
  In praise of life
    And then my daddy gets a knife;
We have our fill
  Of Mister Bread
    And Missus Yam
      And cornlings by the pound,
    And we chop off the head
  Of the Mothernut squash
With her Babynuts gathered around.

And every sip of tea with cream
  Meets our lips with a little scream
    As we wash our dinner down.

4. The Predicament

Jenny said get in the boat
    So I did
But then she got out
    And the kids all flid
       And took my clothes
          And pushed me off
    And now my toes
Are getting froze.

I want to find
Where they all hid,
But this boat only rows,
And slow.

But momma knows
What they did;
    She'll be real sore,
       And send for a tow,
    And I'll have a show

 When they all get
The royal oar.

Sitting cold
  Is such a bore
    And rowing home
  Is such a chore.

I sure hope momma knows.

5. Born with them

I was born with them,
  And anyway they don't look that bad;
  They never stopped me
From playing games,
  Going to school,
    Crafting with my mom,
      Or hiking with my dad.

  He calls them protection,
  Like a helmet or a pad,
  And I can't complain;
    But when you call me goat girl,
    Or demon, or beast,
    And faint, and wail, and call a priest,
  It makes me
Just a little bit sad.

6. We Came to Look

We came along to take a look,
  In our little air machine.

We saw a scene just like a book:
  Sky of blue, and fields of green.

But someone tried to shoot us down.
  We think you folks are pretty mean.

Our fearless leader turned around
  And flew us back to Blunderbean.

7. Catapult

In order to take people
      Fast and far,

They came up with a thing
      We call a car.

And I guess that's really
      Nobody's fault.

But I wish they came up
      With a catapult.

8. Shadow

I don't know when my shadow started snacking,
  But it gained a lot of weight that I don't have;

And now when I go anywhere, it feels like I'm packing
  The shadow of a mountain, or a really heavy bag;

And I just want to drag it to a cliff
  And push it over,
But whenever I approach, it gets too heavy to drag.

It holds me there,
  And we just stare, shin-deep in clover,

    And I tell it to go, and leave me alone,
      But I hear its dark rebuttals in the air,

    And I am swayed,
And then we shuffle home.

9. Brian and the Lion

"You can't always catch a lion,
   To wear it on your head.
Sometimes, you're gonna die tryin'
   If it catches you instead."

And now our friends are all cryin'
   'Cause those were the last words he said
When that lion got hold of Brian.

   But I reckon a cat's alive,
   And a lunatic is dead.

10. Crows

My house is really a mass of crows,
    They mob together and count their toes;
    They sing their woes;
    And dance hellos,
But when they fly, my whole house goes.

Where they fly to, I don't know,
    I wait and clean the feathers, though,
    And scan the sky
    And look up high,
And down to the sea below,

    Waiting for my missing mass of crows.

11. Sky-Face

When I'm in my Crane-Lift-Sky-Face,
  I sit
    And I think about life
    And cheesecake
    And bugs
    And books, and news, and snow.

  And I count all the hairs
    On the heads
  Of the people
Below.

12. Newts

I like newts as much as fruits.
   But some folks don't like newts at all.
They come and crawl
   All over the table and the wall
But that's no reason
   Not to leave them be;
I don't agree
   With smashing them into a greasy ball,
Or dropping them from trees.

13. Doug

Doug,
  You stand there on the rug.
You pretend that your little mug
  Has liquid gold inside,
Or some rare mold,
But I know better.

It's just a bug
  You found outside
Three days ago,
  And you've been hiding him.
You named him Jim.
  And now you want
To put him down
  Your older sister's sweater.

14. Puffy Collared Coats

My uncle and my aunt
  Have these puffy-collared coats
That are very warm
               And large,
And they'll keep you
  From drowning
    If you fall off a boat.

But my uncle and aunt
  Have no need to float.
They live in Kentucky,
  And I have been told
    They used to raise goats.

But now they don't
  Have any goats.
They just have
  Their giant
    Puffy
  Collared
Coats.

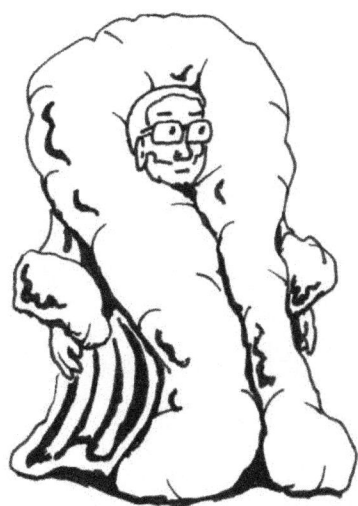

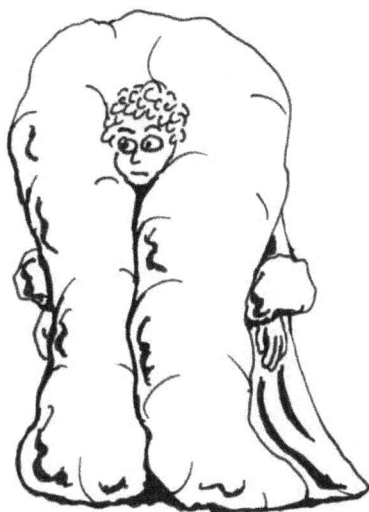

15. Sam in the City

Wait for the right moment, Sam –
   A burst of little bubbles from below.
We've all learned how to dig a clam,
   But here in the city you may not know

How to watch for the bubbles of the sewer man,
   And then bite apart his breathing-hose –
     And be ready when he rises –
      Like a gasping fish that sputters on the land –
   Then you just take his wallet, and go.

16. The Laser

This is what we all wanted:
    A laser that would stop a comet;
Nothing more.

Not a twenty-four
    Foot high monstrosity
        That blasted the whole shore
            Of Miami into dust,
        And left a crater, and some vomit,
    And the remnant of a taco truck
That later fell into the sea.

At least, I didn't want it.

We're the NASA laser folks;
    Preventing craters is our hope.
        So what went wrong?
            I wish I knew.
        I hope the city
    Doesn't sue.

17. Mrs Claire Digley

I went to a luncheon
  Out on a lawn
That Mrs. Claire Digley threw.

And while we were munchin',
  A lady named Gabby
    Conversed with a lady named Sue.

    And they gabbled a bunch, On
      Dickens and Poe,
    And I listened while slurping the stew.

    And as we were brunchin'
      I covered a yawn,
    But Mrs. Claire Digley knew.

So a man with a truncheon
  Asked me to go,
  'Cause I wasn't as polite
As the luncheon-lawn crew.

18. Nutless

I had a nutless dinner
  At a nutless diner
With a nutless winner
  And a nutless whiner.

The winner asked for nutless steak;
  I had a nutless pancake stack;
And the whiner tried his nutless cake,
  Threw a nutless fit, and sent it back.

We all have an allergy,
  And I do not know why-
To certain seeds of certain trees
  And we don't wanna die.

19. The Octopus

Schlup, schlup,
  How do you do?
Schlup, schlup,
  I'm just a visitor,
      Waiting in line,
        I'm just a dude,
    Who needs an ID card.
      Everything's fine,
        Everything's fine.
          Schlup, schlup,
        How do you do?
        Waiting in line,
          Nothing is new.
              I'm planning to go
            To a meeting at two.
            I certainly haven't
            Escaped from the zoo.

20. Can't Think of a Reason

I can't think of a reason
  Not to pee
  and drink
At the same time.

Babies do it
  Happily

So I think
You should be fine.

21. His Shoes

Pots, socks, blocks, and rocks;
I sought to set
  My four collections straight,
    And rate each item;
It was lots of work;
  And getting late.

When **KNOCK KNOCK KNOCKETY KNOCK**
A fancy friend was at the door,
  His name was Nate,
And he just wanted to have a talk;
  A little debate,
About whether and when
  He should take his new shoes
    Back to the store.

I heaved a rock up off the floor,
  And asked him whether he was shore
    He didn't like the shoes,
And **THUD** the rock upon the table
  And turned to hear him say his views
If he was able.

"The shoes are just a little shiny,"
Nate complained,
"And in my brain,
  The strangers that I deal with every day
    Will find them full of frippery,
      And then they might look down on me,
    But I like them every otherwise,
And I don't want to be whiny."

I stared at Nate with a germ of hate
  And wished that I could turn and rate

My rock
   (About a four)
And move on to my pots, socks, and blocks.
   But times like these are ruled by fate,
      And I could not
   Just push him out the door.

"Nate, my fellow, come with me.
   I have a special remedy
      That takes the shine off shoes
         And cars and everything.
      We'll pound them good with a number ten, and boil
them in a six,
   And then you tell me in your view
If there's anything else we need to do
   To get those loafers fixed."

I WHANGED a pot upon the stove
   And hefted the number ten,
But when I turned around I frowned,
   For Nate was nowhere to be found;
      He had hurried home again,
   And I got back to my rocks and blocks,
All muttering and sorting
   In my den.

22. Almost There

My favorite car
  Can go real fast
    And anywhere.

It lifts up
  And goes over the other cars
    Into the air.

Over the grass.
  The ducks are surprised.

Even to space,
  If I close my eyes.

I can take all my friends
  And we can leave our cares
And chase the sweet sunrise.

We're close...
  We're almost there.

23. Some Shapes are Better than Others

My mommy is a triangle,
My daddy is a square.

But no one loves a trapezoid;
They find me hard to bear.

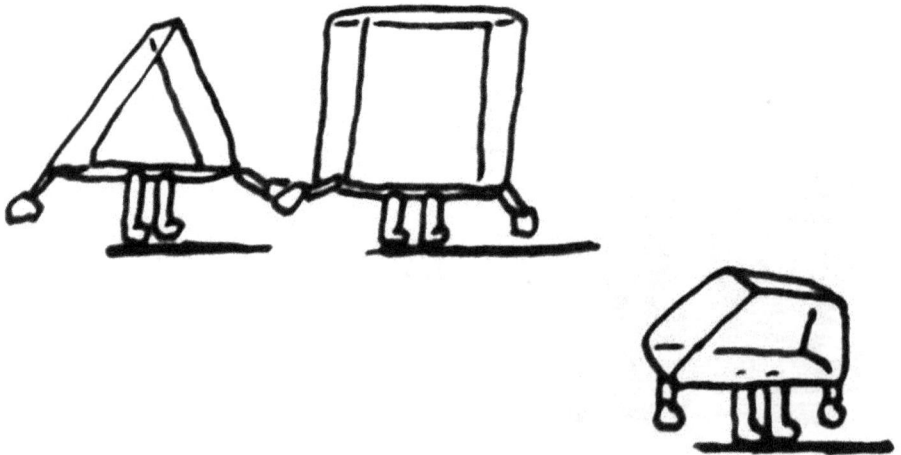

24. A Bird That Can Fly

I'm not going to lie:
  I can't understand
  Why a bird that can fly,
Would sleep in the sand.

  I would sleep in a tree,
    To see all the land;
  Or sleep on the sea,
And drift with my clan.

  And where would I be,
    And where would I go?
The answer's for me
  And my feathren to know.

25. Highway

This
  Has always
    Been
      My dream:

A moving
  Highway
    In the sky

That's made
  Of jet planes
    Flying by

In one
  Continuous
    Stream.

26. My Dad Turned Into a Dog

My dad turned into a dog,
  And I don't know the cause.

But he could always sleep anywhere-
  A couch, a floor, a ratty chair-

And he was a policeman,
  So he talked sharp-
    A little like a bark.

But he really loved
  To pal around,
    And slap your back,
And go to the park.

I think he was tired
  Of enforcing laws.

He was always good
  At sniffing out food;
    So I guess he landed
      A pretty great thing
    When his hair grew out
And his hands became paws.

  Now instead of
    Putting folks behind bars,
      He yaps at them,
    Or wags his tail,
And chases after cars.

27. The Wheezing Worm

Eighteen weighty women
  Wondered why the wind was warm;

Then eighteen weighty women
  Realized with some alarm

That all eighteen of them
  Had wandered
    Where the waiting Wheezing Worm

Lives and lurks and wheezes
  Breathing silent heavy breezes
(To deceive us,
  And to please us with their perfume)
Til a weighty snack appears
  (Sometimes weeks, sometimes years).

Well! the women clucked with pity
  As the Wheezing Worm ate Biddy
    And they jumped with great displeasure
When its flashing teeth took Heather-

She was chewy, she was gooey-

And the sixteen weighty ladies
  Ran away before Miss Louie
    Could be gooey too!

Sixteen substantial souls
   Held a meeting then and there:

Should they fight the fearsome Wheezing Worm;
   Alight its face in flame?
   Or send a hail of heavy rocks
      Around its tentacles and mane?
   Or should Matilda, Sue, and Hilda
      Offer up their buxom builds
      As a distraction of deliciousness
      While thirteen others try to stick
   A spear into its brain?

No, Matilda said
   And Sue and Hilda shook their heads.
     And so
   The weighty women said a prayer
For Heather and Biddy
   And got out of there.

Nobody stays
   And nobody fights
     And this is why
   The Wheezing Worm
Still lies in wait
   Each night.

28. A Tree on a Balloon

I can't say that you can't grow
  A tree on a kite,
    Or a balloon,
And send it up to five thousand feet
  Where it looks like a small green moon.

  And captures heat,
  And captures sun,
  And makes new air
    For everyone you know,
      And love-

Without the nuisance
  Of being there
    Beside you on the ground;

The tree is safer up above,
Where no one chops it down-

In fact, I think you ought to do it soon.

29. Only Three Stars

If there were only three stars in the sky
  We'd all know their names
    And their legends.

One would be "Northy"
  And one would be "Southy"
    And one would be "Saint Eggins. "

There'd be only one constellation
  -The Trinitycorn-
And as far as mythology goes,

There'd be one story arc
  With three clear threads
    Over only three episodes.

Maybe most games
  Would be for three players,

Maybe most cakes
  Would have three layers.

Three sided churches
  (The church of St. Eggins)
With three sided steeples;
  (And three sided cars!)
Three sided doors,
  -You'll love those hinges-
And three-sided people!

In a world with only three stars.

30. The Trip

I was gonna
  Take a trip
And fly so far away,

But the airplane
  Left without me,
So now I have to stay.

31. The Sump-Thing

There's a gurgling noise from under the house;
  Daddy says the space is clear
    And the pump is fair,
But Mommy suggests a giant mouse,
  And sighs, "well,
    SOMETHING'S down there."

I think she's righter than she knows;
  The Sump-Thing lives beneath the floor
    Beneath the stairs;
And eats the dust that falls from our toes,
  Down through the cracks,
    And he tries our wigs,
      And puts on airs.

32. Just a Plant

I know you'll say
  I'm just a plant.
    Can I help it if
      I want to dance?

My merry stem
  Is nothing fancy
    But I'm feeling
      Just plain prancy!

33. National Nonsense Day

I'd like to live in a country
  Where all the leaders play,
And the flag is raised to double-staff
  On National Nonsense day.

And down at the Royal Post,
  They make airplanes out of the mail;
And at the Department of Justice,
  They use a trampoline instead of scales.

You can crawl wherever you need,
  Because they cover the streets with rugs;
And if you need a little comfort
  You go to the Ministry of Hugs!

The national song is one loud BONNNGG
  And we hear it played on the twelfth of May
Over and over, loud and long,
  On National Nonsense Day.

34. Stuck Here

Standing out in my sunny backyard
  With bare feet in the grass
I got the notion that I could ALMOST feel the green blades
  Growing up between my toes.
And so to make a try of it, I stayed there with a garden hose
  To drink from,
And a basket of sweet rye breads,
  And my mother left me out there
    To see how far I would go.

Time passed.
  Time passed.
And now I'm stuck.

Grass, grass, grass, grass,
  It grows between my toes and tickles.

Fast, fast, fast, fast,
  The birds alight. (Sometimes they bite.)
  Their feathery touch is fickle.

Kids crash all past
  Tweak my nose,
And hide around my knees;

I like the breeze;
  I watch the swaying of the trees;
But,

Can't scratch my back,
  Can't do it.

Rain won't help
  And kids don't climb there.

Cats will sometimes sit
  Like little princes
    On the spot
      But it doesn't help the way it should.

Lightning scratched it once,
  Twenty years ago,
    And that was really good.

35. Chickens

Chickens are hard to catch, they said.
  They can't even fly,
    But they run like incredible darts.

Don't go chasing them with your legs.
  Don't even try.
    They'll trip you and peck at your parts.

Leave it to me, I won't slip,
  or die.
    I'm the king
      Of the chicken-catching arts.

36. Winter

Winter is the most bearless* time
   To hike
 And commit hairless crimes
    Like
  Stealing from a sleeping bear
    A bike
   That's parked outside his lair.

But if you dare,
 Then be prepared
  To pedal the heck out of there.

Though the tires be airless,
 The way be steep,
  The trails be careless,
   The snow be deep;

  You'll still have miles to go
 Before
You sleep.

---

* Some bears wake during hibernation. Don't steal from bears.

37. Power Outing

Instead of an outage,
  Mom likes to say:
"We're having a power outing today."

We stride merrily,
  Down the long lane
To buy buckets and pliers;

Because there are
  Fat fallen trees
On the utility wires.

38. The Spectacular Hat Family

Your hat is your helmet, my mother says.
Your hat is your strength and your pride.
But every time I put it on,
I feel like I want to hide.

My family are daredevils, stuntmen and loons.
My father eats glass, my sister reads notes
Flung past her face on poison-tipped darts
By trained little monkeys riding on goats.

My mother breathes fire and hangs from a wire-
Above a loaded powder keg-
And she takes a breath and waves her hand
And calls me over to swing from her legs.

And they all wear a pointed hat like mine.
Tall and protective hats they adore.
I love them all, but I'm starting to think
I don't want to wear my hat anymore.

39. Mr. Henley

Mr. Henley likes to walk
    Upon a tightened wire,
While his wife gives a little talk
    About the thrill,
  The danger,
  And the skill
That it requires.

She tells the crowd to toss their pennies
    And say a little prayer

And watch Mr. Henley jump up in the air.

"Throw them higher than the wire!
  He'll collect them!
  He can get them!
    It's a trick he learned
      While working at the fair!"

But I didn't see him jump,
  Maybe he was having a bad day,
Or maybe
  Mrs. Henley
    Is a liar.

40. The Parakeet

Once upon a Friday deep
  While I tried in vain to sleep,
I heard an ominous little cheep.
  I looked, and saw a parakeet.

He fluttered up around the door
  And grimly glared at my decor,
As if he'd seen it all before
  And wished to see it nevermore.

"Were you blown in from the beach?"
  I cried, "or driven by the sleet?
What business causes us to meet?"
  "Nothing," said the parakeet.

He fixed me with a knowing look,
  And dripped a dropping on my books,
And baldly strutted like a crook,
  Always glaring from the nook

Above the door above the stair;
  Dark and heavy hung the air.
We had a silent standoff there,
  Until I shouted "it's not fair

"For you to come here in the heat
  Of night and give a fearsome tweet,
And stare at me and glare at me
  With all the threat of an angry sea,

"Will you tell me what it means?
  Am I to die like a sardine,
Skewered from the glassy green,

"By the deadly little beak,
  Of a bird who thinks that he can speak??

"Or does it mean that all my dreams
   Will bloom like mold across a cream?

"My art be seen, my stories read,
   My thoughts be flown in all the heads
Of all the people near and far,
   And one day carried to the stars?

"Give me an answer, so I can sleep!!"
   With this I leaped up to my feet,
And thought the bird might want a treat.
But -
   "Nothing," said the parakeet.

And then the birdie flew away.
   And I must wonder to this day
If all our books and all our writing,
   Wins and losses, deaths and cheats,
All our sad and fruitless fighting,
   Are *nothing* to a parakeet.

41. The Mission of the Meeks

"This is the Mission of the Meeks:
  Find a meal for the clan to eat.
    And remember this wisdom as you crawl:
  A cake feeds one, but a human feeds all!"

42. Storywood Pole

I'm telling a story that nobody hears,
  Except for my cousin who lives in a hole,
And writes down my words when they enter his ears,
  And I sit with my back to a storywood pole.

And some people watch from the side of the trail,
  And some of them mutter, and some of them play,
But nobody sits to hear the tale,
  They hem and they haw and they wander away.

When cousin Bernie reads it all back,
  Sometimes we think that it's taken a bend
From the story we liked, so Bernie will smack
  And jiggle the pole, and we'll try it again.

43. Lucy Found a Dragon

Lucy found a dragon,
  Lucy was alone.
Lucy had a wagon,
  So Lucy brought him home.

Mommy's out the window,
  Daddy went away,
Brother ran to Grandma's,
  Just the dragon stayed.

44. The Bridge

I found a bridge to planet Mars;
  I strolled and pondered at the stars.
    I walked for days and months and years
  I thought about my dreams and fears.

There were dancers on the stairs
  At times,
    And ladies selling wares.
  I stopped to sleep,
    I stopped to eat,
      I stopped to rest my weary feet.

It got to feeling very far;
  So I went back home and got a car.
    Eight thousand years is fine for you,
      But I have better things to do.

45. The Bag of Badgers

Grandpa gave me a bag of badgers
  That had been my uncle Tom's.
But cousin Peter swiped it once
  And left it on the lawn.

And a lot of little badgers
  Ran into the grass that day
Because the merry rains of May
  Had frightened them away.

And when I got the dried-out bag
  I looked inside to see,
Just a few tenacious badgers
  Were left inside for me.

GRANDPA

46. Whales

Nowadays on the road you find
  The whales in their giant glassy cars
All full of water,
  Traveling from sea to sea
    On little visits, and fishing trips
With sons and moms and daughters.

I don't really know why the people made
  The cars that whales could drive;
It seems like extra work to me,
  When most of us just want to stay alive.

And really I think we all assumed
  The cars would just confuse them,
But when you give cars to animals,
  It turns out they will use 'em.

47. Different Kinds of Eggs

It seems fairly clear
  To those of us with legs,
    That those of us without 'em
      Came from different kinds of eggs.

48. Marvelous Spa Vats

Toasty, soaky, soapy toes.

Lively liquid lapping at my knees
  And at my never-knows.

Lovely lovely lung-water
  Makes me calm.
    Nothing matters.

A simple sudsy warm solution
  Puckers all my lucky skin parts.

    Pricey, yes. But worth the cash.

  Suckers out there walk around,
    Wasting time on solid ground
      Never knowing what we've found.

Perfect peace worth every penny.

Haven't any care to call him.
  Feeling sound. Feeling fair.

    And haven't any deed to dare.
    I'm not going anywhere.

Love it here.
  Just you and me

And a button-man named Benny.
But I don't see him.
  Did he flee?

   I don't have any clothes with me.
    And now I think (do you agree?)

I think Benny
  Took the key.

49. The Thing About Shelly

This is the thing about Shelly:
  She wanted the fanciest clothes;
    With gold and silk
  And monograms,
     And those socks that hug your toes.

But this was the problem with Shelly:
  She stole a lot of money,
    So the police came along,
     And threw her in jail,
And her cellmates just think she looks funny.

50. Bat Bacon

Look. I've never had bat bacon.
  And no, I'm not on a diet.

But I'm not exactly achin'
  To pick it up and try it.

51. Outside This Box

Outside this box is a great baboon
  Who tells you tales from his perch on the moon,
  And waits to welcome everyone
When their time in the box is done.

"No! Outside the box is an empty space
  Like a giant oven, ready to bake
  A million cakes or a million pies,
  To bring tears of joy
To a million children's eyes."

These could be myths, they could be lies.
  I've never looked outside the box
    To see the truth
  (Although I've tried)
    And neither have you.
  But I think when we make it out of here
We'll probably all be surprised.

www.ingramcontent.com/pod-product-compliance
Lightning Source LLC
Chambersburg PA
CBHW051846040426
42447CB00006B/725

* 9 780692 617809 *